FREDERICK COUNTY PUBLIC LIBRARIES

Rookie biographies®

Franklin D. Roosevelt

By Wil Mara

Consultant
Nanci R. Vargus, Ed.D.
Assistant Professor of Literacy
University of Indianapolis, Indianapolis, Indiana

Children's Press®
A Division of Scholastic Inc.
New York Toronto London Auckland Sydney
Mexico City New Delhi Hong Kong
Danbury, Connecticut

Designer: Herman Adler Design
Photo Researcher: Caroline Anderson
The photo on the cover shows Franklin D. Roosevelt.

Library of Congress Cataloging-in-Publication Data

Mara, Wil.
  Franklin D. Roosevelt / by Wil Mara.
    p. cm. – (Rookie biographies)
Summary: An introduction to the life of the thirty-second president, Franklin D.
Roosevelt, whose three terms in office spanned the years of the Depression and
the Second World War.
Includes bibliographical references and index.
  ISBN 0-516-21844-1 (lib. bdg.)   0-516-25823-0 (pbk.)
  1. Roosevelt, Franklin D. (Franklin Delano), 1882-1945–Juvenile literature.
  2. Presidents–United States–Biography–Juvenile literature. [1. Roosevelt,
Franklin D. (Franklin Delano), 1882-1945. 2. Presidents.] I. Title. II. Series:
Rookie biography.
  E807.M28 2004
  973.917'092–dc22

2003013690

©2004 by Scholastic Inc.
All rights reserved. Published simultaneously in Canada.
Printed in the United States of America.

CHILDREN'S PRESS, and ROOKIE BIOGRAPHIES®, and associated
logos are trademarks and or registered trademarks of Scholastic Library
Publishing. SCHOLASTIC and associated logos are trademarks and or
registered trademarks of Scholastic Inc.
1 2 3 4 5 6 7 8 9 10 R 13 12 11 10 09 08 07 06 05 04

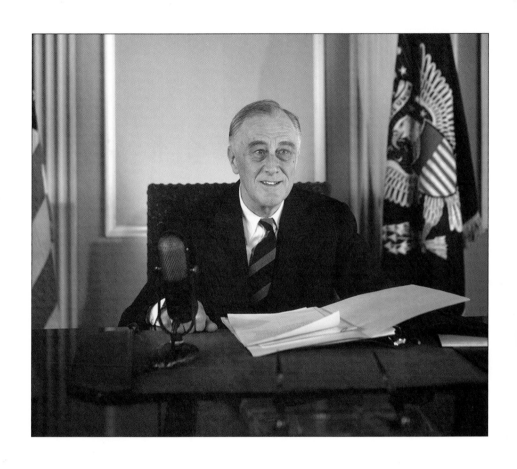

Franklin D. Roosevelt was the thirty-second president of the United States.

Roosevelt was born on January 30, 1882, in Hyde Park, New York. His family was rich.

For many years, Roosevelt went to school at home. His family taught him to care about other people.

Roosevelt met his wife,
Eleanor, in college.

Eleanor worked with poor
people in New York. She cared
about other people, too.

Roosevelt had a famous cousin. His cousin was Theodore Roosevelt. Theodore was the twenty-sixth president of the United States.

Theodore Roosevelt

Franklin D. Roosevelt

Theodore helped Roosevelt
to decide to run for office.
Roosevelt thought he could
help many people this way.

In 1910, Roosevelt ran for senator (SEN-uh-tor) in New York. He won.

A senator is someone who helps make laws.

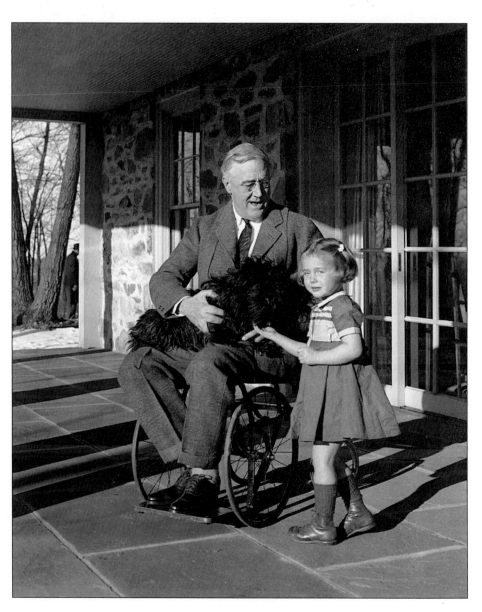

In 1921, Roosevelt got sick. He got a disease called polio (POH-lee-oh).

After that, he had to use a wheelchair. That did not stop his work.

In 1928, people in New York made Roosevelt their governor (GUHV-uh-nor). A governor runs a state.

Roosevelt did a good job. He helped many people who did not have jobs.

Roosevelt became president of
the United States four times.

The first time was in 1933.
Many people could not find
work at that time.

Roosevelt found ways to
help these people.

Slowly, things began to get better. Then Roosevelt had another problem to solve.

In 1941, the United States joined a war. The country fought against Japan, Germany, and Italy.

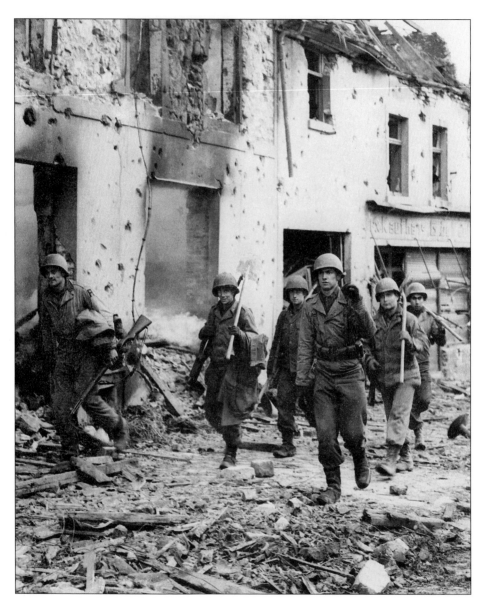

The United States worked with
other countries to win the war.
Many people died. It was
a sad time.

In 1945, Roosevelt became president for the fourth time.

By this time, Roosevelt was very sick from many colds. Yet he kept working to end the war.

Roosevelt went to his home in Georgia to rest. He died there on April 12, 1945.

The war ended soon after Roosevelt died.

Roosevelt was a great president.

Words You Know

run for office

polio

president of the United States

senator

Theodore Roosevelt

Index

About the Author

More than fifty published books, including biographies, bear Wil Mara's name.
He has written both fiction and nonfiction, for both children and adults. He lives
with his family in northern New Jersey.

Photo Credits

Photographs © 2004: Brown Brothers: cover, 25; Corbis Images: 3, 7, 10, 17, 22, 30
top right, 30 top left (Bettmann), 13, 14, 30 bottom, 31 left; Franklin D. Roosevelt
Presidential Library and Museum: 6, 26; Hulton|Archive/Getty Images: 5, 18; North
Wind Picture Archives/Nancy Carter: 29; Superstock, Inc/The Huntington Library:
9, 21, 31 right.

2 1982 01550 1640

APR 1 9 2005